How to Leverage Gen Z Preferences in Marketing Strategies:

A Reliable Resource for Common Challenges.

Dr. Zuleyka Colon Colon

Dedications:

I would like to dedicate this work to those who have faith in me and support my aspirations and endeavors. My sincere gratitude goes to the Lord for providing me with strength and guidance to overcome the numerous challenges along my journey. To everyone who purchases and reads this book, I express my heartfelt thanks and hope it proves valuable in helping you make informed decisions in your business pursuits.

Contents

Chapter I:

Gen Z Preference for Advertising and its Impact on Purchasing Intention

Single-clickable images have been a widely used marketing strategy in online advertising for many years. Tech giants like Alphabet (Google), Amazon, and Microsoft have championed this approach. However, fluctuations in the economy, uncertainty in these times, and the changing purchasing preferences of Gen Z have disrupted the advertising landscape. This has led businesses to acknowledge the importance of fostering closer customer relationships and prioritizing content creation (Singh et al., 2022, p. 7). Hence, Fidelity Investments and other investment firms are shifting their focus to Gen-Z investors through different social media platforms; TikTok is one notable example. On this platform, billions of views have been recorded on posts that are related to the field of investment, which demonstrates the keen interest of this younger demographic in this area. In order to effectively reach this audience, established companies offer reliable information and valuable interaction on social media platforms so a foundation of trust can be built. However, concern persists that abundant online guidance could lead to inappropriate investment decisions. Hence, to avoid any such case, firms are striving to modify their approaches and foster trust among the clients of the younger generation by providing tailored and personalized services (Sim, 2021).

In contrast to online advertising, content marketing provides firms with a wider range of opportunities to engage their target audience more effectively (Toit, 2022). By establishing a smart rapport with their customers, businesses can deliver value that resonates with them (Hilton et al., 2020, pp. 366, 368). To accomplish this, firms can integrate their social media presence with customer success management (CSM) to enhance their marketing endeavours (Wibowo et al., 2021, pp. 13-15). While a dearth of creativity in marketing can pose a hurdle, it is a crucial aspect of the journey towards offering value to customers.

The research conducted on Gen Z sheds light on this generation, born after 1996, which has been deeply influenced by economic fluctuations and historic downturns (Strozniak, 2022). They have been exposed to technology and the internet early, making them highly aware of all digital mechanisms (Singh et al., 2022, p. 8). Compared to previous generations, they have a lower attention span and are more impatient to focus on one task or device at a time (Grigoreva et al., 2021, p. 170). Furthermore, Gen Z values personal and professional growth, lives quickly, and prefers buying products primarily on social media platforms, spending most of their time actively using those platforms (Singh et al., 2022, p. 18). The rapport of businesses with this generation on social media significantly impacts their purchasing intentions (Singh et al., 2022, p. 18) and decisions (Grigoreva et al., 2021, p. 164). This generation values rapport and quality of information, making the abundance of information supplied in content marketing a magnet for them (Singh et al., p. 8).

Problem

As advertising may not consistently align with the needs of businesses or customers. The objective of this study is to gather data and assess the effectiveness of investing in advertising for implementing customer success management (CSM) among Gen Z. CSM is a strategy that emphasizes the quality of customer experience to maximize value. Furthermore, the study also aims to determine the impact of CSM on influencing purchasing decisions. Hence, the objective is to prove that content marketing is more effective in engaging this young generation and building lasting relationships between them and investment firms. Additionally, this study seeks to demonstrate that content marketing provides a better return on investment and consistently drives demand for firms.

Technological development has revolutionized how products and services are accessed, causing significant changes in consumer and business behaviours. With this transformation comes a new marketing era, where online sales have surpassed traditional marketing channels due to the rise of mobile phones, tablets, and other technological devices (Pomirleanu et al., 2022, p.170). Moreover, the growth of social media and social networking research has led to increased data marketing articles and data collection. This shift has even garnered attention in journals outside the marketing field, demonstrating the widespread impact of these advancements (Pomirleanu et al., 2022, p. 171).

In recent years, content marketing has slowly evolved, with upcoming advancements that feature lengthy content, a shift towards quality and consistency, the development of influencer marketing ecosystems, and a renewed emphasis on ROI and attribution (Nite, 2018), the impact of technology has significantly transformed the marketing landscape. In order to maintain competitiveness, organizations must embrace new technological advancements. Digital marketing can potentially increase reach and target specific audiences, but it also raises concerns about data privacy and ethical advertising practices. Over the years, ethical considerations have emerged regarding internet advertising, such as truth in advertising and avoidance of harmful stereotypes. Unethical marketing practices can erode consumer trust and damage brand reputation. However, content creation has brought about change by providing opportunities for better business-to-consumer (B2C) relationships.

Objective

This project aims to address the shifting market dynamics and consumer behaviour, specifically focusing on the demographic of influential Gen Z. Due to rapid technological advancements and changing purchasing habits, businesses must adapt their strategies to remain successful. The project aims to propose effective solutions that enable businesses to understand and engage with Gen Z while capturing their attention, ultimately leading to increased and consistent demand generation, sales, and a positive return on investment. The decision to target Gen Z is grounded in recognizing their significance as a consumer group with unique preferences and values. Hence, the urgency of this initiative stems from Gen Z's current shaping influence on market trends, and by addressing these challenges now, businesses can gain a competitive edge in adapting to evolving market demands.

Research Question

Is online advertising or content creation more effective in driving Gen Z's purchasing intentions?

Chapter ll

Literature Review

In the 21st century, marketing theory has become increasingly crucial as Gen Z has access to more information about products and services (Fromm & Read, 2018, p. 16), making it easy for them to be distracted by several options available. Additionally, businesses need to take a deep look back at the evolution of marketing and create strategies based on relevant findings and inferences from innovative marketing investigations. This is because resistance to change can cause a business to become obsolete, and fail to adapt to changing generational needs.

The feasibility of marketing across channels has increased competition across sectors, both internally and externally. In a digital era, where Gen Z shares value with millennials but increasingly demands evidence and input, working towards trusting relationships is highly beneficial for businesses and customers. The need for relations in marketing was noticed before the 21st century and has now evolved, including new competencies and increased values. As tracking interactions were not enough, businesses recognized the need to supply quality experiences to customers and accept their contributions toward developing products and services. The past steps brought marketing towards the concept of customer success management, which prioritizes relationships consistently to meet the demands of the digital-savvy generation, Gen Z. However, image ads alone are insufficient to drive traffic and create demand. Overall, the evolution of relation marketing and Gen Z's frequent changes may be driving forces toward content creation and might be a factor in the purchase decision.

In today's business landscape, marketing theory is more crucial than ever, particularly when it comes to reaching the Gen Z demographic. This generation has unprecedented access to information and is constantly bombarded by offers from various companies, making it imperative for businesses to stay ahead of the curve (Fromm & Read, 2018, p. 16); especially those that fail.

To evolve, a business must mitigate the risk of becoming obsolete. To succeed, companies must analyze the latest marketing research and use innovative strategies to connect with their audience (Fromm & Read, 2018, p. 17).

While digital channels have made it easier for businesses to connect with consumers, they have also led to increased competition both within and outside of sectors. Gen Z consumers share values with millennials but are more discerning and require input and evidence. This way, building strong relationships with customers becomes a key factor in business success.

Relationship marketing has evolved to include new competencies, emphasizing the maximization of value rather than merely tracking interactions. Today, businesses recognize the importance of delivering exceptional customer experiences and accepting customer contributions to product and service development (Hilton et al., 2020, p. 362).

The latest evolution in marketing is customer success management, which prioritizes building relationships to meet the needs of the digital-savvy Gen Z demographic. However, a simple image advertisement is no longer enough to generate demand (Wibowo et al., 2021, p. 14). The evolving relationship between businesses and consumers, combined with Gen Z's preference for content, has made content creation a critical factor in purchase decisions.

In the realm of advertising, maintaining consistent content marketing is imperative. However, if advertising firms fall short in this regard, businesses can greatly benefit from adopting marketing strategies that prioritize consistent customer success management. This approach helps gather relevant metrics and inspires innovation and demand creation (Laitkep et ala., 2021, p. 2). To be more specific, catering to customers' unique desires and needs can generate demand, particularly when targeting the Gen Z demographic. This generation is known for their willingness to experiment with new products and offer valuable insights, which can help.

Create services and products that align with their immediate purchasing preferences (Grigoreva et al., 2021, p. 170). In today's digital age, social media platforms offer an effective way to reach a wide audience. Visual content creation has become the primary focus of campaigns, replacing single pay-per-click image ads (Grigoreva et al., 2021, p. 170).

The ease and affordability of creating independent content have driven the growth of e-commerce businesses, sales, and marketing across multiple internet-connected devices (Grigoreva et al., 2021, p. 165). Nowadays, businesses partner with influencers to craft content that showcases their products or conveys their message on social media platforms such as Instagram and YouTube. These frequent communications remain online for extended periods, increasing brand awareness and recognition (Singh et al., 2022, pp. 8, 17, 18). Unlike single pay-per-click ad campaigns, which may not get traffic due to various factors such as ad blockers or users lacking time to click, sustained exposure to services and products can foster brand recognition. However, changes in data privacy laws among technology devices have empowered users to refuse tracking, making it challenging for companies to obtain relevant metrics (Brinson et al., 2018, p. 136).

Furthermore, Gen Z's short attention span (Grigoreva et al., p. 170) makes it unlikely for them to pay attention to pay-per-click advertising. Some may even view this type of advertising as a threat to their devices. Although they are tech-savvy, they do not tend to click impulsively, as firms may assume. Grigoreva et al. (2021) argued that "Gen Z places great importance on reviews and desires to be involved in business processes" (p. 166). Therefore, it is essential to explore motivators such as online advertising and content marketing (content creation), the two primary focus areas. Customer success management relies heavily on customer engagement and experience, both of which are essential components in the development of customer relationships.

To ensure a valuable customer experience, continuous innovation and customization of products and services are imperative (Hilton et al., 2020, p. 368). Gen Z constitutes a significant proportion of online purchases, so they pose a challenging group to satisfy (Grigoreva et al., 2021, p. 166). Investigating whether online advertising or content marketing has a greater impact on purchase decisions is important. Hence, this study is gaining momentum in determining the most efficient and effective advertising method to win over Gen Z and build relationships crucial for brand success.

The research focuses on the investment industry, which has emerged as a significant area of concern, particularly in the wake of the recent economic upheaval associated with Gen Z. As a result, there is a growing demand for financial expertise, which has become a necessity in the 21st century (Sconti, 2022). On social media platforms, Gen Z is targeted with tailored content marketing, a tactic businesses and influencers use to create concise yet impactful multimedia messages throughout the product and service cycle (Grigoreva et al., 2021, p. 170). This content is accessible online and can be revised and updated, which may entice Gen Z to return for more.

Modern advertising has taken a new form with content marketing, which utilizes popular social media platforms like Instagram, Facebook, and YouTube to showcase engaging and informative content about products and services. This approach is continuously updated, providing mutual benefits for the customer and the firm. Singh et al. (2022) noted that "it offers greater control over products, services, and marketing" (p. 9).

To effectively engage with Generation Z, it is vital to integrate impactful content into your Customer Success Management (CSM) strategy. CSM builds upon the foundation of Customer Relations Management and is particularly critical when connecting with a generation that has unrestricted access to information (Singh et al., 2022, p. 8). To establish a meaningful

rapport with this demographic, it is important to prioritize and comprehend their needs. CSM champions e-commerce reliance and underscores the value of enabling customers to test products and services (Hilton et al., 2020, p. 363).

The literature utilized in this review is notably pertinent to the study's targeted demographic and temporal context. In addition, it presents promising prospects for future research, given the rapid advancements in technology and marketing. As part of customer success management strategies, marketers are tasked with developing compelling content that facilitates the attainment of customer objectives (Singh et al., p. 17). Meanwhile, the investment sector may serve as a model for further initiatives to empower customers to achieve their goals. Notably, more literature on the efficacy and efficiency of social media marketing by investment firms targeting the Gen Z cohort is needed.

The current study explores the pertinent topic of Generation Z's decision-making process regarding investments in the United States. Its purpose is to bridge the gap in representation and shed light on the steps taken by this population to make informed decisions (Grigoreva et al., 2021, p. 164). This research aims to provide investment firms with opportunities to enhance their client's success by creating compelling content that captures Gen Z's attention and fosters long-term relationships (Strozniak, 2022, pp. 1-2). Fintech firms have an edge in this area, given Gen Z's high awareness of financial technology compared to millennials worldwide (Mohannad et al., 2020, p. 21). Nonetheless, this study aims to identify the type of advertising that truly resonates with and retains Gen Z Americans as customers of traditional investment services. The competition among investment firms, brokers, financial planners, and advisers for sales and recurring clients makes this an essential area of focus.

Historical Context

This research project explored academic sources from reputable databases such as Google Scholar, ProQuest, and Touro University Worldwide Library. The objective was to establish a comprehensive historical context and to understand the current landscape surrounding the focus of the project. A comprehensive literature review was conducted, primarily focusing on peer-reviewed articles published within the last decade. This timeframe ensures that the information gathered is current and relevant to the rapidly evolving dynamics of the research subject. Various relevant keywords, including but not limited to Generation Z, social media, online marketing, online advertising, and digital content, were strategically employed to perform a meticulous search. The goal of utilizing these keywords was to ensure that the literature evaluation was accurate and comprehensive by capturing diverse perspectives and viewpoints. The use of scholarly materials from reputable databases underscores the commitment to academic rigour and the necessity for reliable data to guide and support research projects.

Conceptual Framework

The conceptual framework of this project provides direction by clarifying the connections between key factors and concepts essential for understanding Generation Z's advertising preferences and their influence on purchasing behaviour. The framework is derived from a thorough analysis of relevant literature obtained from reputable databases such as Google Scholar, ProQuest, and the Touro University Worldwide Library. It integrates findings from research on online advertising, purchase intention, content marketing, and customer success management. The layered flowchart visually represents these interconnected components (Figure 1), which provides an explanation of the conceptual framework.

Beginning with 'Gen Z Preference for Advertising,' the first layer of the flowchart, the subsequent layers reveal a sequence of critical factors influencing purchasing intention. As the diagram illustrates, content marketing serves as a catalyst, shaping Generation Z's preferences and subsequently affecting their purchasing decisions. This is further interconnected with online advertising, creating a complex network of interactions. The inclusion of Customer Success Management signifies the post-purchase phase, highlighting the importance of user satisfaction and retention within the overall framework. As these layers interact, the framework aims to investigate the implications of return on investment (ROI). The findings and analysis derived from this framework are essential for guiding the subsequent discussion and drawing meaningful inferences.

Supporting the Conceptual Framework:

The conceptual framework is underpinned by a synthesis of scholarly sources that delve into Gen Z behaviour, marketing strategies, and the evolving landscape of digital advertising. The project ensures a theoretical foundation that aligns with current knowledge and perspectives by grounding the framework in academic literature. This strengthens the robustness of the conceptual framework and establishes a link between the theoretical constructs and their practical implications. A narrative walkthrough of the flowchart allows the reader to understand how each layer contributes to the overarching research objectives, thereby reinforcing the relevance and coherence of the conceptual framework in supporting the project.

Figure 1

Conceptual Framework

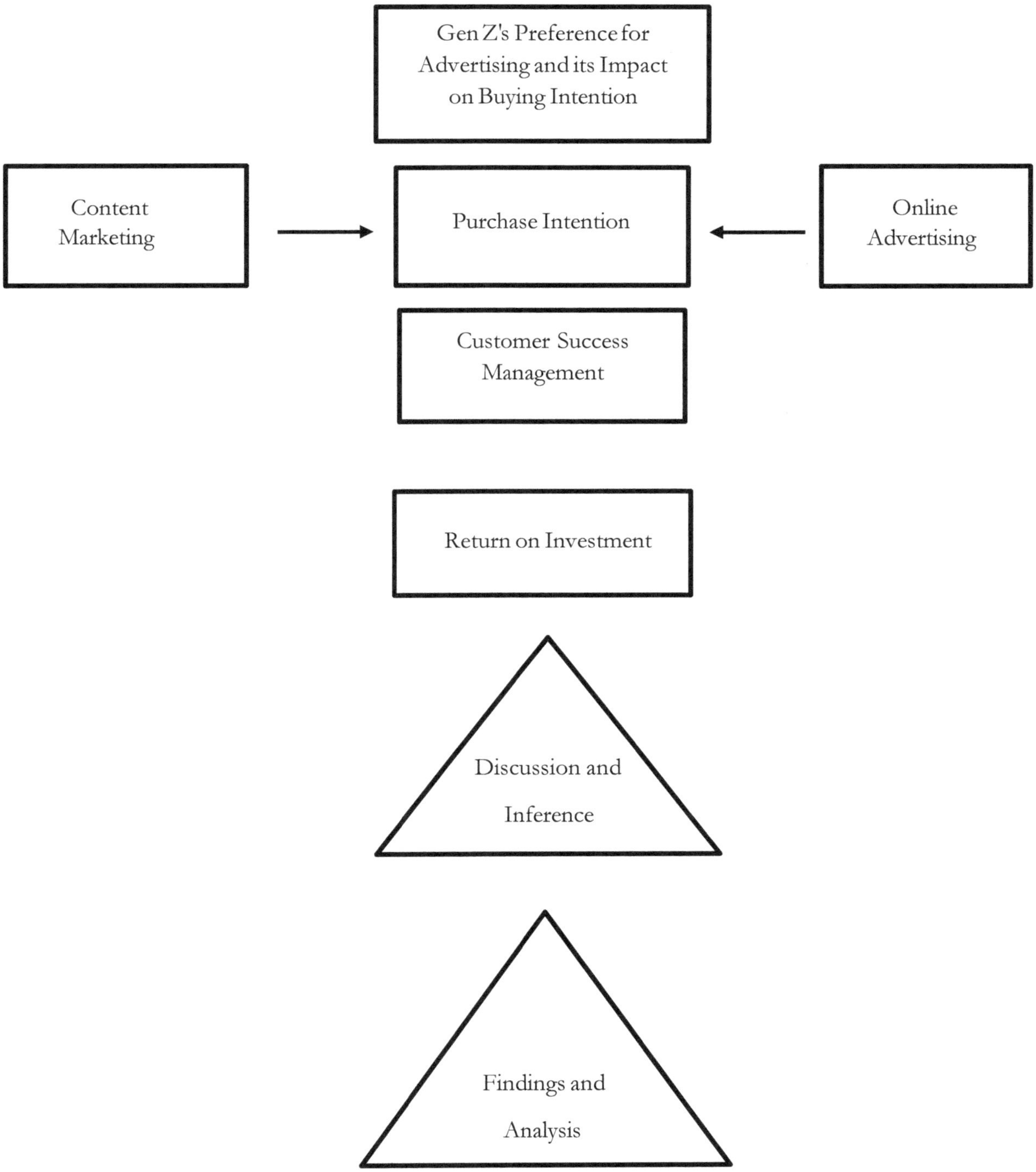

Figure 2

Research Variables

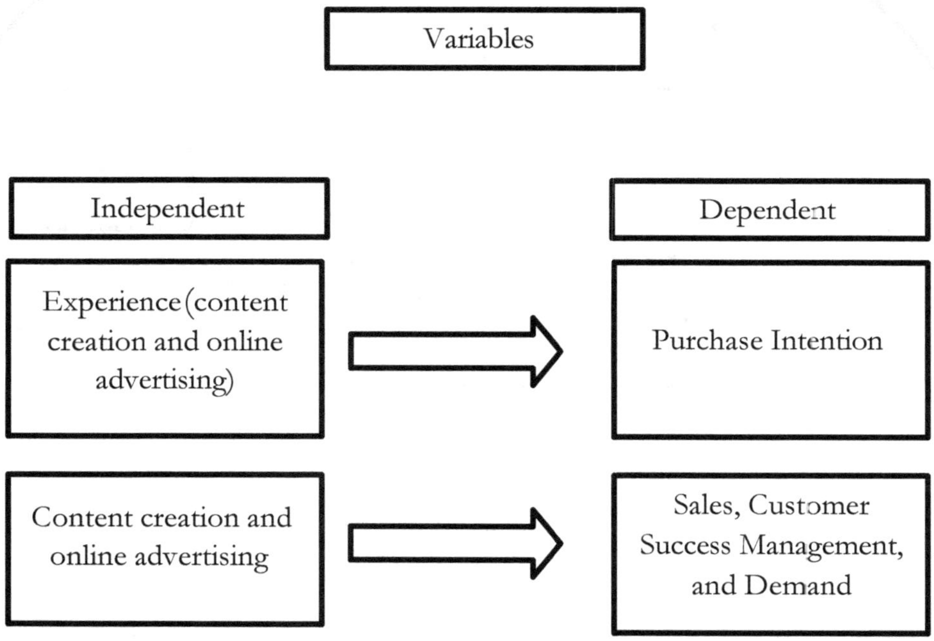

Figure 2 above illustrates the core variables at the heart of this research investigation. On the left, under the category of Independent Variables, the experiential aspects of Generation Z are examined, specifically focusing on their engagement with content creation and online advertising. These variables, labelled 'Experience,' are the driving force to understanding the nuances of Gen Z's preferences and interactions in the digital marketing landscape.

On the right, under the category of Dependent Variables, I explored the outcomes and impacts of Gen Z's experiences. The primary focus is on 'Purchase Intention,' representing the likelihood and inclination of Generation Z to engage in investment services based on their interactions with content creation and online advertising. Additionally, the figure outlines three crucial aspects— 'Sales,' 'Customer Success Management,' and 'Demand.' These variables collectively capture the broader implications and consequences of Gen Z's digital experiences, shedding light on their potential influence on sales patterns, customer relations, and overall demand for investment services. The interconnected nature of these variables forms the foundation of my research, unravelling the intricate relationship between Generation Z's digital experiences and the multifaceted outcomes in the realm of investment services.

Chapter III

Methodology

In this study, a quantitative methodology was employed to collect empirical evidence. This research method was selected for its suitability in measuring and analyzing a large sample size, providing statistical data and enabling the generalization of findings.

Quantitative research was selected as the most suitable methodology for investigating purchase intention, as it allows for the measurement and analysis of numerical data. This approach reveals patterns, trends, and relationships among variables, providing precise and reliable results that contribute significantly to understanding purchase intentions among the Gen Z demographic. The insights and conclusions drawn from this approach are relevant to the business problem at hand. The research is centered around people born after 1996, also known as Generation Z. This technique offered invaluable insights into the behavior and preferences of this specific demographic group.

In September 2023, a survey was conducted to gather insights from members of Generation Z who are familiar with internet browsing and social media platforms.

SurveyMonkey's targeted responses were utilized for participant recruitment to ensure that only eligible participants were included. The survey comprised multiple-choice questions and a Likert scale ranging from "strongly agree" (5) to "strongly disagree" (1). With 626 respondents, a margin of error of ±3% was permitted, and the survey achieved a complete response rate.

The primary goal of the study was to assess the efficacy of investing in online advertising campaigns compared to utilizing content variations in social media messages to establish and maintain customer success management among Gen Z. The ultimate objective was to achieve a higher return on investment and foster a culture of demand and innovation in business. The survey questions were tailored to financial investment services, reflecting Gen Z's objectives and interests in investment opportunities.

The survey utilized an anonymous response system that maintained participant confidentiality while allowing feasible tracking of participation. Geographical verification was performed through the IP address without any personal identification or risk involved. All collected data were securely processed through a trusted system, as stated by Loh (n.d.). Thus, the survey conducted for this investigation did not threaten the participants. For this research, the data collection in this research was carefully structured, beginning with the establishment of objectives and development of a plan. SurveyMonkey was selected as the survey platform due to its practicality and data export features for analysis. A pre-validated survey from a prior marketing study was adapted, with permission from its authors, and modified to align with study variables before being submitted for IRB review.

Upon obtaining the required authorization to collect data, targeted responses were purchased through SurveyMonkey. Notably, a 100% completion rate was achieved within a remarkably short period of two days, with participants averaging just 3 minutes and 11 seconds to complete the survey, surpassing the estimated completion time of over 10 minutes. While initial authorization involved minor adjustments for relevance and alignment, no further pilot testing was conducted due to the rapid and comprehensive response rate obtained during the main data collection phase.

Data Collection

The collected data was rigorously formatted for analysis, ensuring consistency and organization throughout. The investigative instrument, designed to gauge perceptions and intentions, incorporated the Likert scale and multiple-choice statements. To prevent potential biases, the survey structure was carefully tailored to capture Generation Z's immediate responses. Notably, this phase emphasized the survey's utility, which, in addition to employing predetermined statistical techniques, offered valuable features such as insights and trend analysis.

Statistical Tests

Multiple regression was conducted using SPSS software to assess the relationships between this study's independent and dependent variables. The independent variables consisted of Content Marketing on Social Media and Online Advertising, while the three dependent variables were Purchase Intention, Investment, and Demand for Investment Services. According to Field (2018), multiple regression predicts a continuous dependent variable based on multiple independent variables. Multiple regression also allows the researcher to determine the model's overall fit (variance explained) and the relative contribution of each of the predictors to the total variance explained. Four sets of hypotheses were tested:

H_{01}: Gen Z's experience with content marketing does not significantly affect purchase intention.

H_{11}: Gen Z's experience with content marketing positively affects purchase intention.

H_{02}: Gen Z's experience with online advertising does not significantly affect purchase intention.

H_{12}: Gen Z's experience with online advertising positively affects purchase intention.

H_{03}: Content marketing on social media platforms does not substantially contribute to enhancing sales or strengthening the relationships that investment firms have with Generation Z, particularly when compared to the effectiveness of online advertising.

H_{13}: Content marketing in social media platforms has a bigger role in increasing sales and strengthening investment firms' relations with Gen Z than advertising.

H_{04}: Online advertising is less effective in generating demand for investment services than content marketing among Gen Z.

H_{14}: Online advertising is more effective in generating demand for investment services among Gen Z than content marketing.

A few assumptions must be satisfied before performing multiple regression. Linearity and homoscedasticity will be assessed by visually examining the scatter plots of the standardized residuals and the standardized predicted values. No violation of the linearity assumption is present if the plots are not curved (Field, 2018). Furthermore, the homoscedasticity assumption is not violated if the plots exhibit a rectangular pattern (Field, 2018). The Shapiro-Wilks test will be conducted to determine whether the data are normally distributed (Field, 2018). Kurtosis and skewness values will be computed to further evaluate normality. According to Hair et al. (2010) and Byrne (2010), data is considered normally distributed if the skewness falls between -2 and +2 and the kurtosis falls between -7 and +7. Lastly, to determine whether multicollinearity between any two variables has been broken, the variable inflation factor (VIF) will lastly be computed for each variable (Field, 2018).

At the 5% level, statistical significance will be evaluated. The corresponding coefficients (b1, b2, b3, etc.) are considered statistically significantly different from zero if the p-value is less than or equal to 0.05. Conversely, if the p-value is greater than 0.05, there is no significant difference between the corresponding regression coefficients and zero. This would imply that no meaningful relationship exists between the corresponding independent variable and the dependent variable. The detailed discussion and interpretation of the findings will be further elaborated in Chapter 4.

The regression model was selected as a valuable tool to analyze the relationship between the selected predictors and dependent variables. This methodology utilizes the intercept formula to predict the dependent variable (Y) based on the independent variables (X). The coefficients derived from the regression analysis were then interpreted to evaluate the effects of online advertising and content marketing on the respective dependent variables. For instance, the impact of online advertising on the demand for investment services was assessed. The use of regression analysis is particularly appropriate for this project, as it allows for a nuanced examination of how changes in the predictors influence the dependent variables, thereby providing valuable insights into the dynamics of the relationships.

Linear regression, a statistical technique employed in this research, examines the relationship between an independent and dependent variable. The process involves gathering data for both variables and visually assessing patterns through plotting. The intercept formula was applied to fit the data points, and the R-squared value, ranging from 0 to 1, was calculated to measure the goodness-of-fit. The t-statistic was then compared to a critical value to determine the significance of the slope, and conclusions were drawn about the relationship between the dependent and independent variables. While linear regression may be time-consuming, its effectiveness lies in establishing statistically significant differences between content marketing choices and online advertising on dependent variables such as purchase intention, demand, customer success management, and sales. These differences were crucial for establishing content marketing as a more effective choice when competing against online advertising. The detailed results and interpretations stemming from these analyses will be presented in Chapter 4.

Survey Instrument

Gen Z Preference for Advertising and its Impact on Purchasing Intention

The survey was crafted as part of a doctoral project to enhance the understanding of Gen Z's preferences regarding investment service advertising and purchasing decisions. A power analysis was conducted using G*Power to determine the minimum required sample size for the study. Four criteria were considered during the power analysis: significance level, test power, effect size, and statistical technique. The likelihood of rejecting a null hypothesis is the significance level, sometimes referred to as Type I error (Haas, 2012). Usually, quantitative research uses a 95% confidence level because it provides adequate statistical support for a test (Creswell, 2013). According to Cohen (1977), the effect size is the approximate measurement of the variables' relationship and is divided into three categories: small, medium, and large.

According to Berger et al. (2013), researchers usually use a medium effect size because choosing a small effect size is too lenient, and a large effect size is too lenient. The test's power is the possibility of correctly rejecting a null hypothesis (Sullivan & Feinn, 2012). An 80% power is typically used in quantitative studies.

Multiple regression was employed as the statistical test in this investigation. To perform multiple regression and detect a medium effect size at the 5% significance level with 80% power, a minimum of 68 participants was required. Participants were greeted with an introductory message outlining the purpose of the research and assuring them of the voluntary nature of their participation. The message included the estimated time for survey completion (10 to 15 minutes) and emphasized the commitment to privacy and data protection.

The survey instrument, which functioned as a key data collection tool, was designed to address specific aspects of Gen Z's preferences in investment service advertising. It included questions related to purchasing decisions, advertising content, and factors influencing decision-making. The survey's structure and content were carefully aligned with the research problem outlined in Chapter 2, ensuring their relevance to the study objectives.

A comprehensive review process was conducted to ensure that the questions effectively captured the intended constructs, thereby enhancing the validity of the survey instrument. Face validity, content validity, and construct validity were considered during the design phase to confirm that the instrument accurately measured the intended variables. Reliability was ensured through the use of established scales, and internal consistency measures were implemented to verify the instrument's reliability. The survey's design sought to reduce biases and errors, contributing to the overall robustness of the data collected.

If modifications were made to the original survey instrument, this section outlines what was modified, why the modifications were necessary, and their potential impact on reliability and validity. The modified instrument underwent testing to ensure its effectiveness in accurately capturing the intended data. This testing process included pilot studies or pre-testing with a small sample to identify and address any issues before the full-scale survey administration. This section provides a comprehensive overview of the survey methodology, focusing on the instrument's characteristics, validity, reliability, modifications, and testing processes within the context of the research project.

Content marketing (creation) is the practice of designing effective sensory communications during the products and services cycle (Grigoreva et al., 2021, p. 170). It utilizes social media platforms such as Instagram, Facebook, and YouTube to present sensory information about a product or service, and is regularly updated.

Online advertising is the strategy that firms use to drive online sales. It typically appears in the form of clickable images that direct users to a website. However, it lacks creativity and is not recognized as a tool for brand awareness or customer engagement (Toit, 2022).

Social Media Marketing

ENT1 I purchase investment services on social media because of content marketing.

ENT2 I purchase investment services on social media because the contents shown are interesting.

INT1 I purchase investment services on social media because it allows me to share information with others.

INT2 I purchase investment services on social media because it is possible to have a conversation, comment, and share.

INT3 I purchase investment services on social media because it is easy to deliver my opinion.

TRN1 I purchase investment services on social media because the contents shown are up to date.

TRN2 I purchase investment services on social media because they show the latest product information.

CUS1 I purchase investment services on social media because they offer customized information searches.

CUS2 I purchase investment services on social media because it provides customized services.

WOM1 I'm willing to pass along information on the brand, product /services from social media to my friends.

WOM2: I'm willing to upload or repost content from social media on my blog or social media /microblog.

Customer Experience

SEN1 The social media investment content tries to engage my senses.

SEN2 Participating (e.g., commenting, sharing) on social media investment content is very interesting.

FEL1 The social media investment post tries to put me in a certain mood.

FEL2 The social media investment content makes me respond emotionally.

THK1 The social media investment content tried to intrigue me.

THK2 The social media investment content stimulates my curiosity.

ACT1 The social media content tries to make me think about my lifestyle.

ACT2 The social media investment content reminds me of activities I can do.

REL1 The social media investment content tries to get me to think about relationships.

REL2 I can relate to other customers through social media investment content.

Relationship Quality

SAT1 How satisfied are you with shopping for investment services on social media?

SAT2 How satisfied are you with the relationship created through investment content on social media?

SAT3 Overall, I am satisfied with the investment services on social media.

SAT4 I am pleased with the experience of purchasing investment services from social media.

SAT5 I think purchasing investments from social media is a good idea.

SAT6 Overall, I am satisfied with the experience of purchasing services/products from social media.

TRU1 Social media investment content can be relied upon.

TRU2 Social media investment content is trustworthy.

TRU3 I have complete confidence in the social media investment content.

TRU4 If I required help, the representative on social media would do his/her best to help me.

TRU5 Overall, promises made by the representative on social media are likely to be reliable.

TRU6 The investment representative on social media performs his/her role very well.

Purchase Intention

INT1 I am likely to purchase investment services on social media.

INT2 I recommend purchasing investment services on social media in the future.

INT3 I will likely purchase investment services on social media.

INT4 I am likely to make a particular investment in social media.

Loyalty Intention

LYL1 I will purchase another investment service offered by social media in the future.

LYL2 I will encourage/recommend friends and relatives to use the investment service offered by social media.

LYL3 I intend to stay with social media as my preferred investment space.

LYL4 I intend to recommend social media to others.

Intention to Participate

INP1 Whenever I see a post from social media that I enjoy, I would "like" the content.

INP2 Whenever I see a post from social media that I like, I would "comment" on the content.

INP3 Whenever I see a post from social media that I like, I would "share" the content.

INP4 It is worth sharing, commenting, and selecting "like" on social media.

INP5 I'm willing to provide my experience and suggestions when my friend wants to buy investment services in social media.

INP6 I'm willing to recommend which investment is worth buying in social media to my friend.

Chapter IV

Hypotheses & Findings

This research examined the value of investing in online advertising for customer success management (CSM) among Gen Z and its influence on their buying decisions. The primary objective was to demonstrate that content marketing is a more effective approach to engaging this young generation and establishing enduring relationships between them and investment firms. Additionally, the study sought to illustrate that content marketing offers a superior return on investment and consistently drives demand for financial firms. What follows is a detailed description of the sample used in this study and a discussion of the results of descriptive and inferential statistics conducted with SPSS software. Descriptive measures consisted of frequencies and percentages for variables measured at the nominal level of measurement and means and standard deviations for those measured at the interval level. Inferential statistics involved performing multiple regression analysis to test the study's hypotheses.

Sample Demographics

There were a total of N = 160 participants in this study, of whom 98 (61.3%) were female and 62 (38.3%) were male (Table 1).

Table 1

Participants' Gender

	Frequency	Percent
Male	62	38.8
Female	98	61.3
Total	160	100.0

The majority of participants' household income fell between \$25,000 and \$49,999, comprising 35 (21.9%) of the sample. This was followed by the \$0 - \$9,999 range with 28 (17.5%) participants, and \$10,000 - \$24,999, with 23 (14.4%) participants. More detailed information on household income is provided in Table 2.

Table 2

Household Income

	Frequency	Percent
$0-$9,999	28	17.5
$10,000-$24,999	23	14.4
$25,000-$49,999	35	21.9
$50,000-$74,999	18	11.3
$75,000-$99,999	21	13.1
$100,000-$124,999	13	8.1
$125,000-$149,999	6	3.8
$150,000-$174,999	3	1.9
$200,000+	3	1.9
Prefer not to answer	10	6.3
Total	160	100.0

Descriptive Measures of Study Variables

The independent variables - content marketing, online advertising, and sales, as well as the two dependent variables - purchase intention and investment, were derived by averaging the survey items corresponding to each study variable. The reliability of each measure was assessed by calculating Cronbach's alpha, a measure of internal consistency. A generally accepted rule is that α of 0.6-0.7 indicates an acceptable level of reliability, and 0.8 or greater is a very good level (Serbetar et al., 2016). Nunnally (1978) recommends a minimum level of 0.7. The Cronbach's alphas for the reach measure were all greater than 0.80, indicating good reliability.

Each measure was based on a five-point Likert scale, ranging from 1 (Strongly agree) to 5 (Strongly disagree). Lower values of each variable indicate a greater level of that construct. Table 3 presents the means and standard deviations for each study variable. The highest mean was for purchase intention (M = 2.97, SD = 1.04), followed by content marketing (M = 2.82, SD = 0.93), online advertising (M = 2.80, SD = 0.83), sales (M = 2.76, SD = 0.81), and investment (M = 2.65, SD = 0.75)

Table 3

Descriptive Statistics of Study Variables (N = 160)

	Minimum	Maximum	*M*	*SD*
Purchase Intention	1.00	5.00	2.97	1.04
Content Marketing	1.00	5.00	2.82	.93
Investment	1.00	5.00	2.65	.75
Online	1.00	5.00	2.80	.83
Sales	1.00	5.00	2.76	.81

Results of Hypothesis Testing

Linear regression was performed using SPSS to test the first hypothesis:

H_{01}: Gen Z's experience with content marketing does not significantly affect purchase intention.

H_{1}: Gen Z's experience with content marketing positively affects purchase intention.

Linearity and homoscedasticity were confirmed, as assessed by a plot of standardized residuals against the predicted values (Figure 3).

Figure 3

Scatter Plot of Standardized Residuals versus Predicted Values (Hypothesis 1)

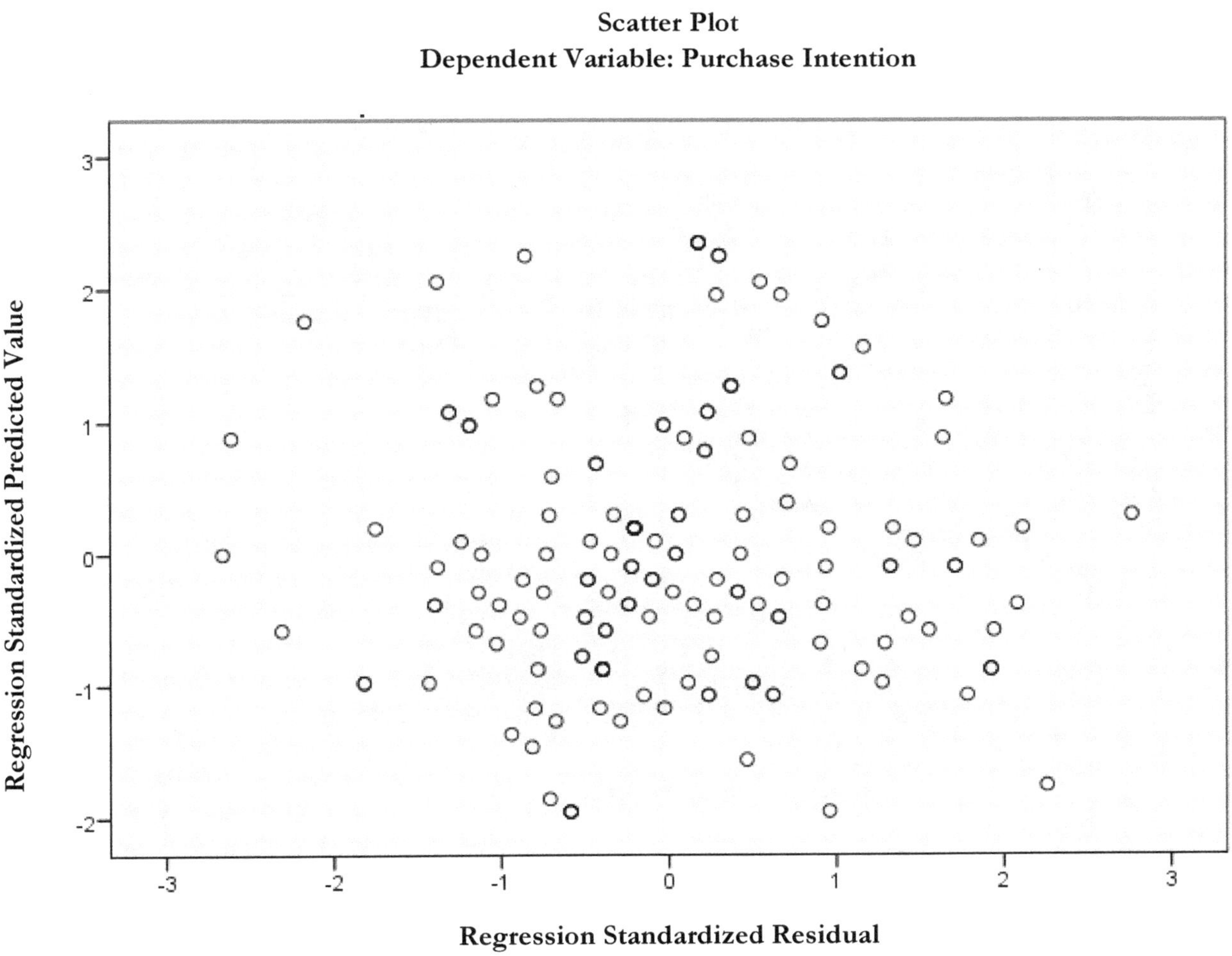

There were no standardized residuals greater than ±3 standard deviations, indicating no outliers. The assumption of normality was met, as assessed by inspection of a histogram of residuals **(Figure 4).**

Figure 4

Histogram of Regression Residuals (Hypothesis 1)

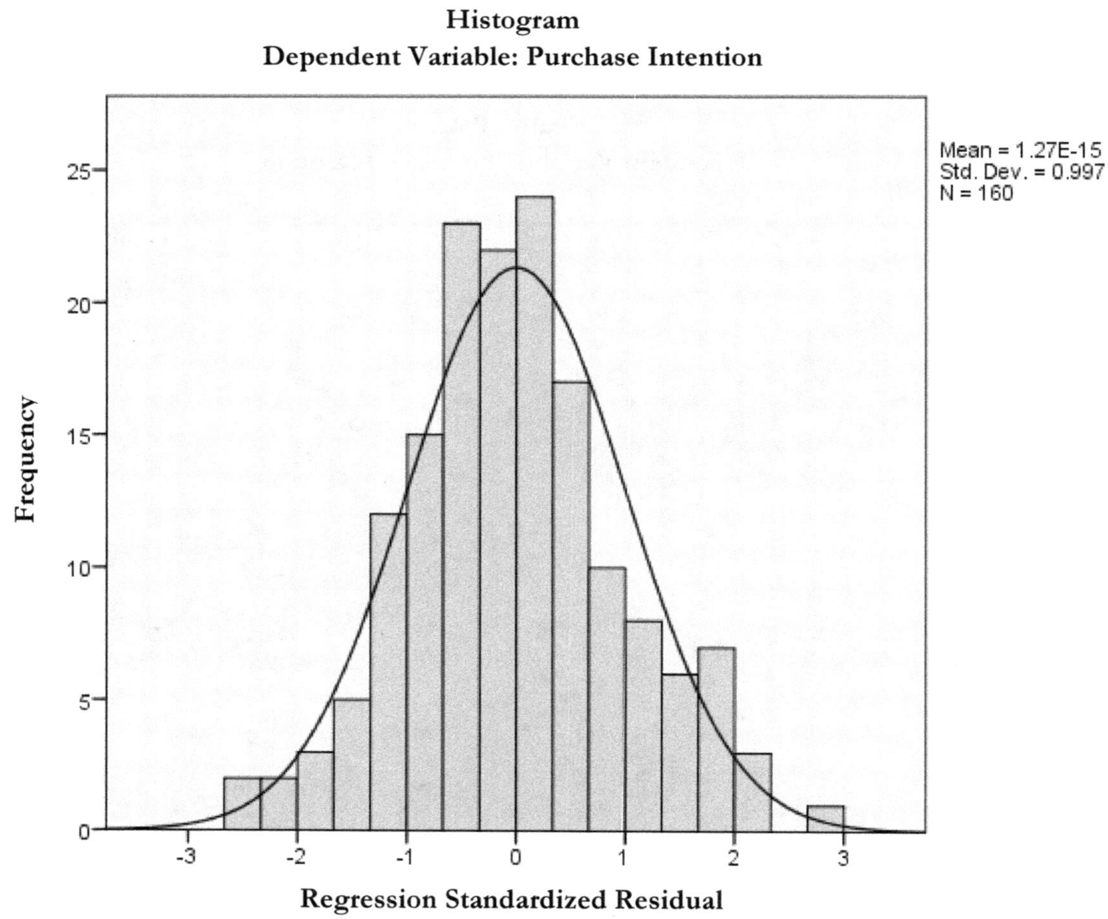

The overall model was significant, F (1, 159) = 251.936, p < .001. The model explained 61.5% of the variance in predicting purchase intention (R^2 = .615). Content marketing was a significant predictor of purchase intention (B = 0.876, p < .001). An increase in content marketing led to a significant increase in purchase intention. Table 4 provides these details.

Table 4

*Regression Coefficients of Regression Model Predicting Purchase Intention from Content Marketing**

	Unstandardized Coefficients		Standardized Coefficients	*t*	*p.*
	B	*SE*	*β*		
(Constant)	.504	.164		3.080	.002
Content Marketing	.876	.055	.784	15.872	.000

$*F(1, 159) = 251.936, p < .001; R^2 = .615$

Linear regression was conducted with SPSS to test this second hypothesis:

H_{02}: Gen Z's experience with online advertising does not significantly affect purchase intention

H_{12}: Gen Z's experience with online advertising positively affects purchase intention.

Linearity and homoscedasticity were present, as assessed by a plot of standardized residuals against the predicted values (Figure 5).

Figure 5

Scatter Plot of Standardized Residuals against the Predicted Values (Hypothesis 2)

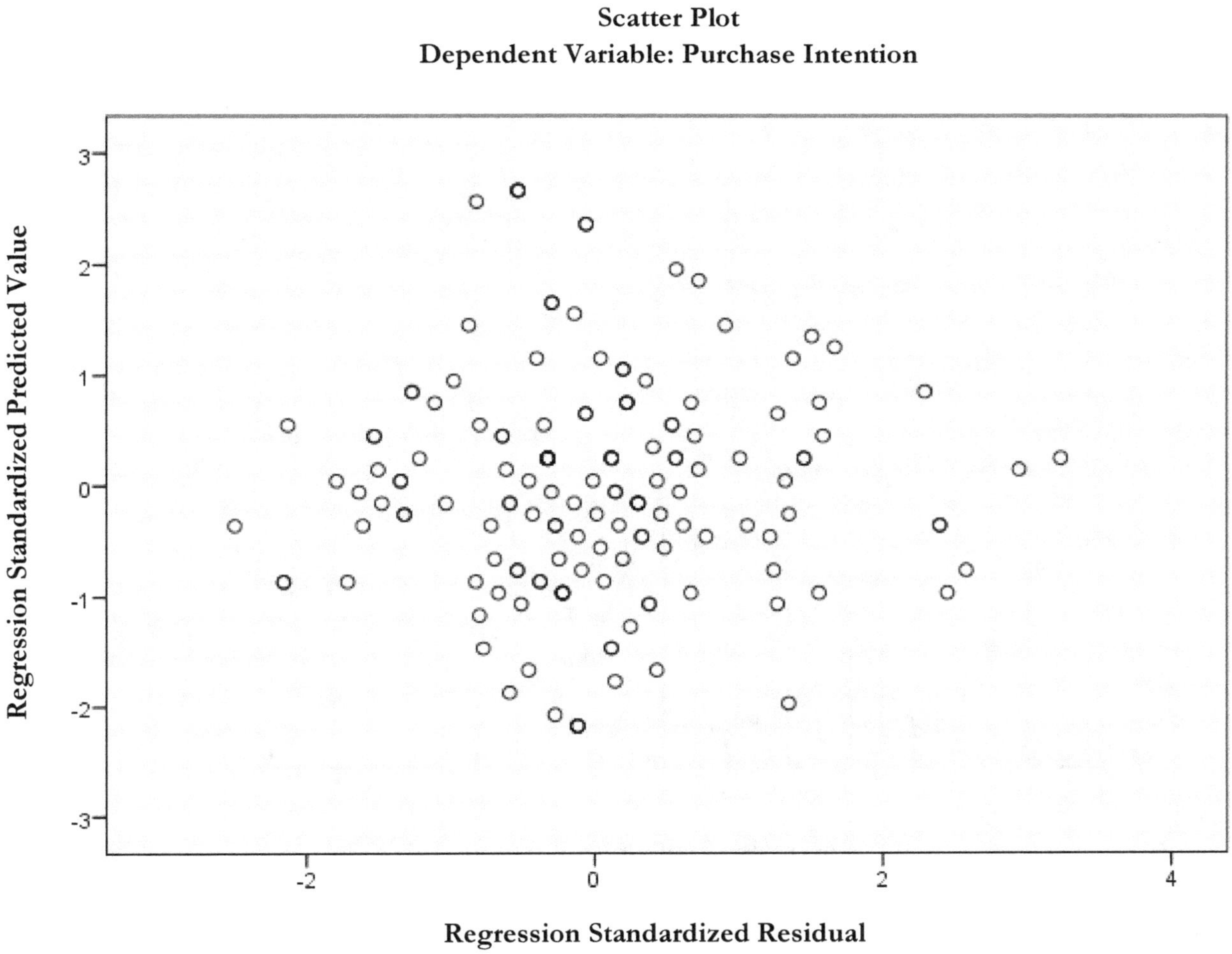

There were no standardized residuals greater than ±3 standard deviations, indicating no outliers. The assumption of normality was satisfied, as assessed by inspecting a histogram of residuals (Figure 6).

Figure 6

Histogram of Regression Residuals (Hypothesis 2)

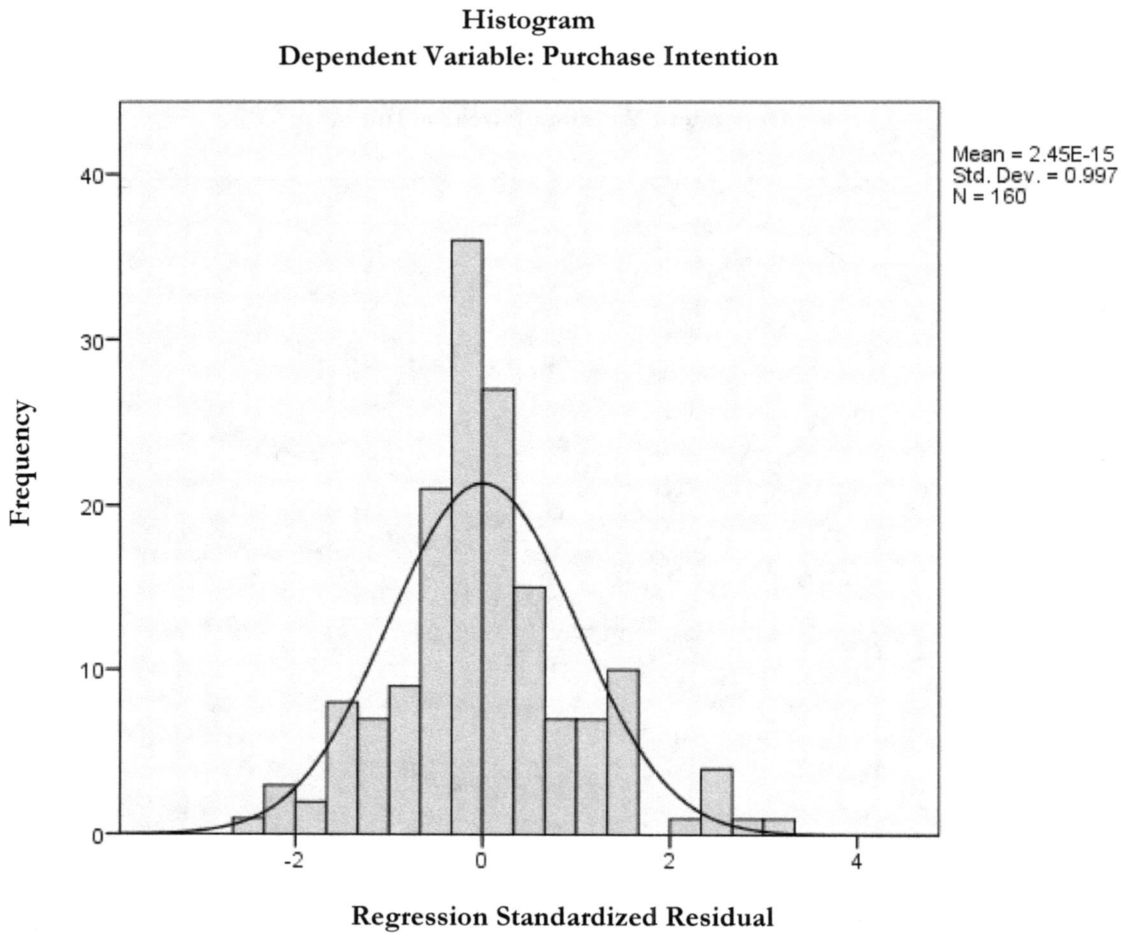

The overall model was significant, F (1, 159) = 384.880, p < .001. The model accounted for 70.9% of the variance in predicting purchase intention (R2 =.709). Online advertising was a significant predictor of purchase intention (B = 1.058, p < .001). An increase in online advertising led to a significant increase in purchase intention. Table 5 presents this information.

Table 5

*Regression Coefficients of Regression Model Predicting Purchase Intention from Online Advertising**

	Unstandardized Coefficients		Standardized Coefficients	t	p
	B	SE	β		
(Constant)	.008	.157		.052	.958
Online	1.058	.054	.842	19.618	.000

**F (1, 159) = 384.880, p < .001;* R^2 *=.709*

Linear regression was conducted with SPSS to address this third hypothesis:

H_{03}: Content marketing on social media platforms does not play a bigger role in increasing sales nor strengthening investment firms' relations with Gen Z compared to online advertising.

H_{13}: Content marketing in social media platforms has a bigger role in increasing sales and strengthening investment firms' relations with Gen Z than online advertising.

Linearity and homoscedasticity were present, as assessed by a plot of standardized residuals against the predicted values (Figure 7).

Figure 7

Scatter Plot of Standardized Residuals against the Predicted Values (Hypothesis 3)

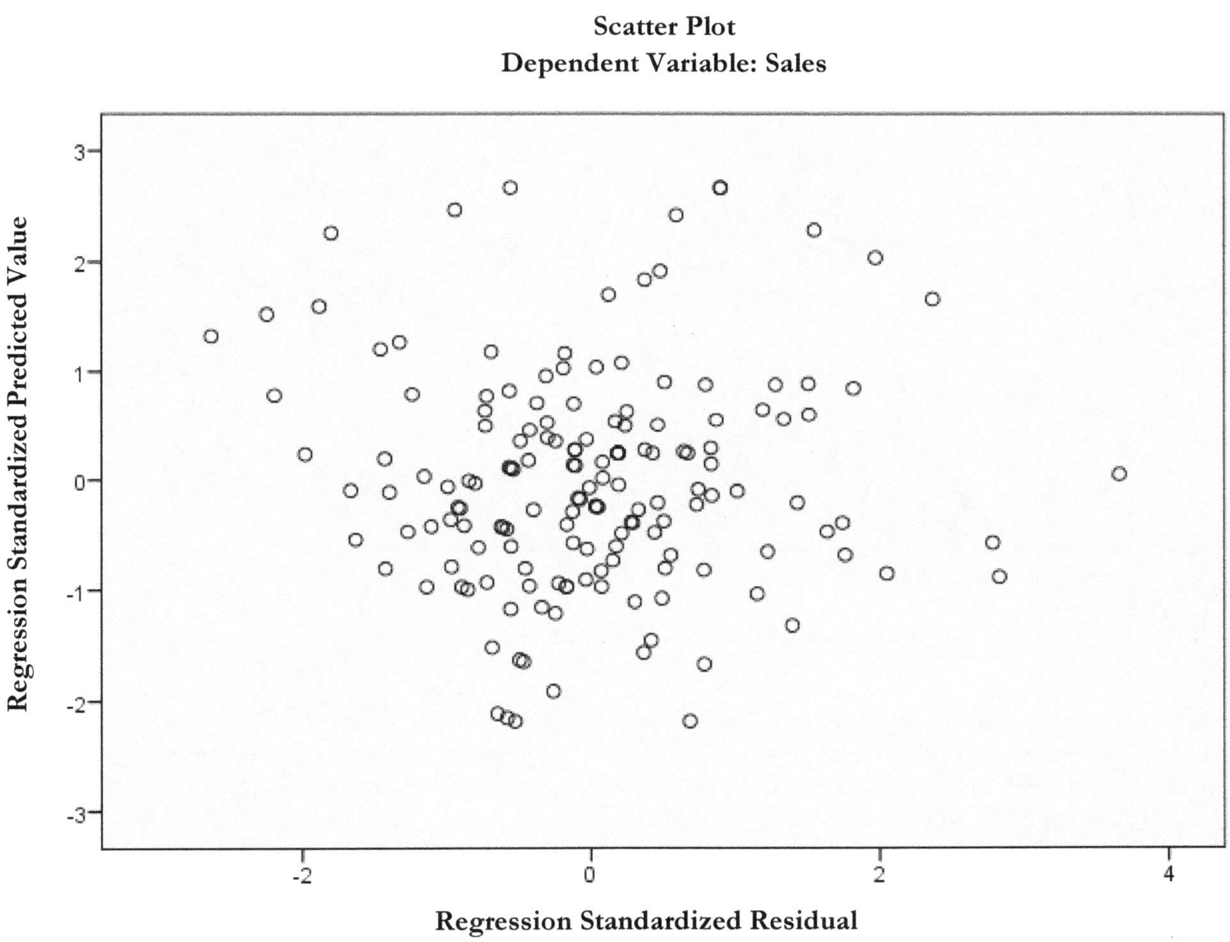

There were no standardized residuals greater than ±3 standard deviations, indicating no outliers. The assumption of normality was met, as assessed by inspecting a histogram of residuals (Figure 8).

Figure 8

Histogram of Regression Residuals (Hypothesis 3)

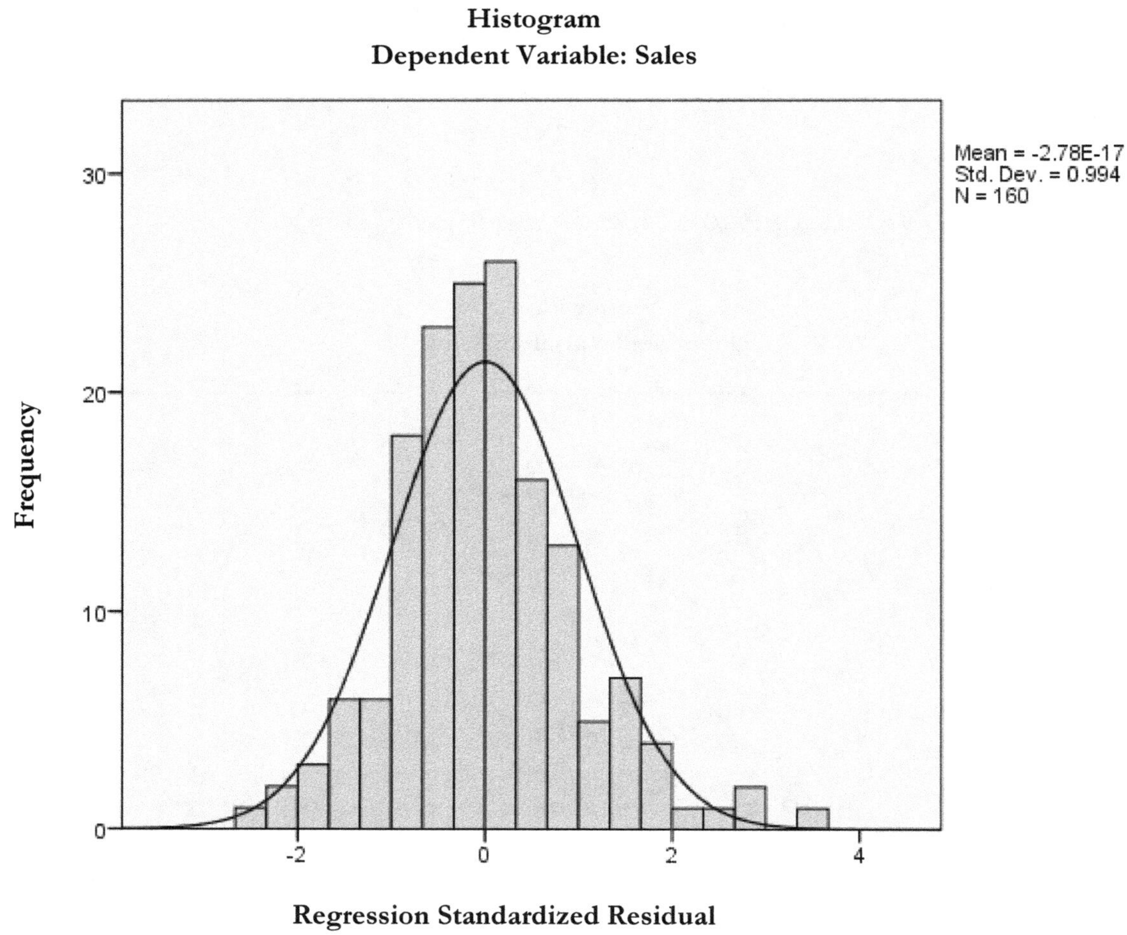

The overall model was significant, F (2, 159) = 230.742, p < .001. The model explained 74.6% of the variance in predicting sales (R2 =.746). Online advertising (B = 0.607, p < .001) and content marketing (B = 0.246, p < .001) were significant predictors of sales. Increases in both online advertising and content marketing resulted in a substantial increase in sales. Table 6 provides this information.

Table 6

Regression Coefficients of Regression Model Predicting Sales from Online Advertising and Content Marketing*

	Unstandardized Coefficients	Standardized Coefficients		*t*	*p*	Collinearity Statistics
	B	*SE*	*β*			VIF
(Constant)	.363	.116		3.124	.002	
Online	.607	.071	.616	8.505	.000	3.241
Content Marketing	.246	.063	.281	3.886	.000	3.241

*$F(2, 159) = 230.742, p < .001; R^2 = .746$

Linear regression was conducted with SPSS in order to address this fourth hypothesis:

H_{04}: Online advertising is less effective in creating demand for investment services than content marketing among Gen Z.

H_{14}: Online advertising is more effective in creating demand for investment services among Gen Z than content marketing.

Linearity and homoscedasticity were present, as assessed by a plot of standardized residuals against the predicted values (Figure 9).

Figure 9

Scatter Plot of Standardized Residuals against the Predicted Values (Hypothesis 4)

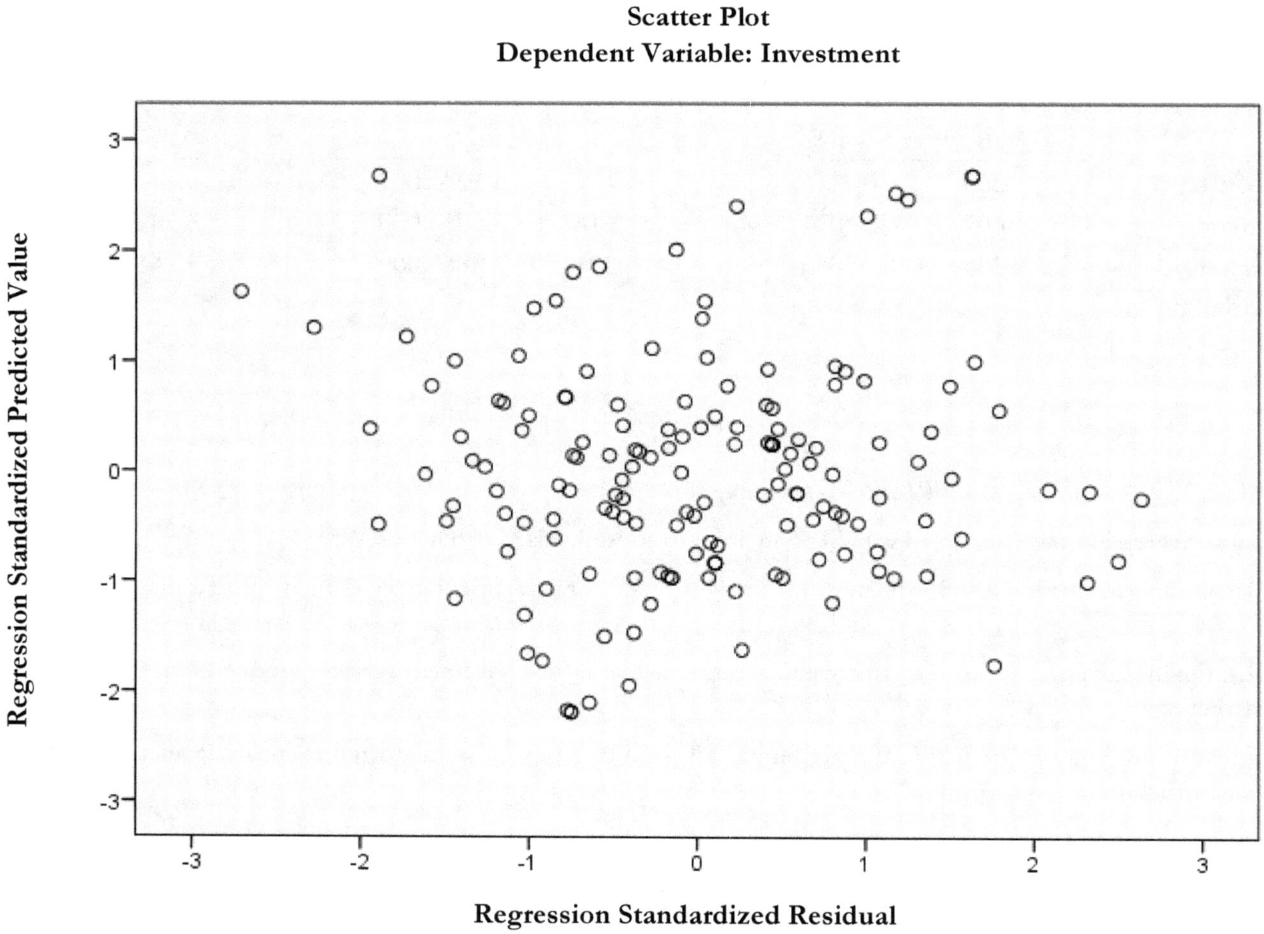

There were no standardized residuals greater than ±3 standard deviations, indicating no outliers. The assumption of normality was met, as assessed by inspection of a histogram of residuals (Figure 10).

Figure 10

Histogram of Regression Residuals (Hypothesis 4)

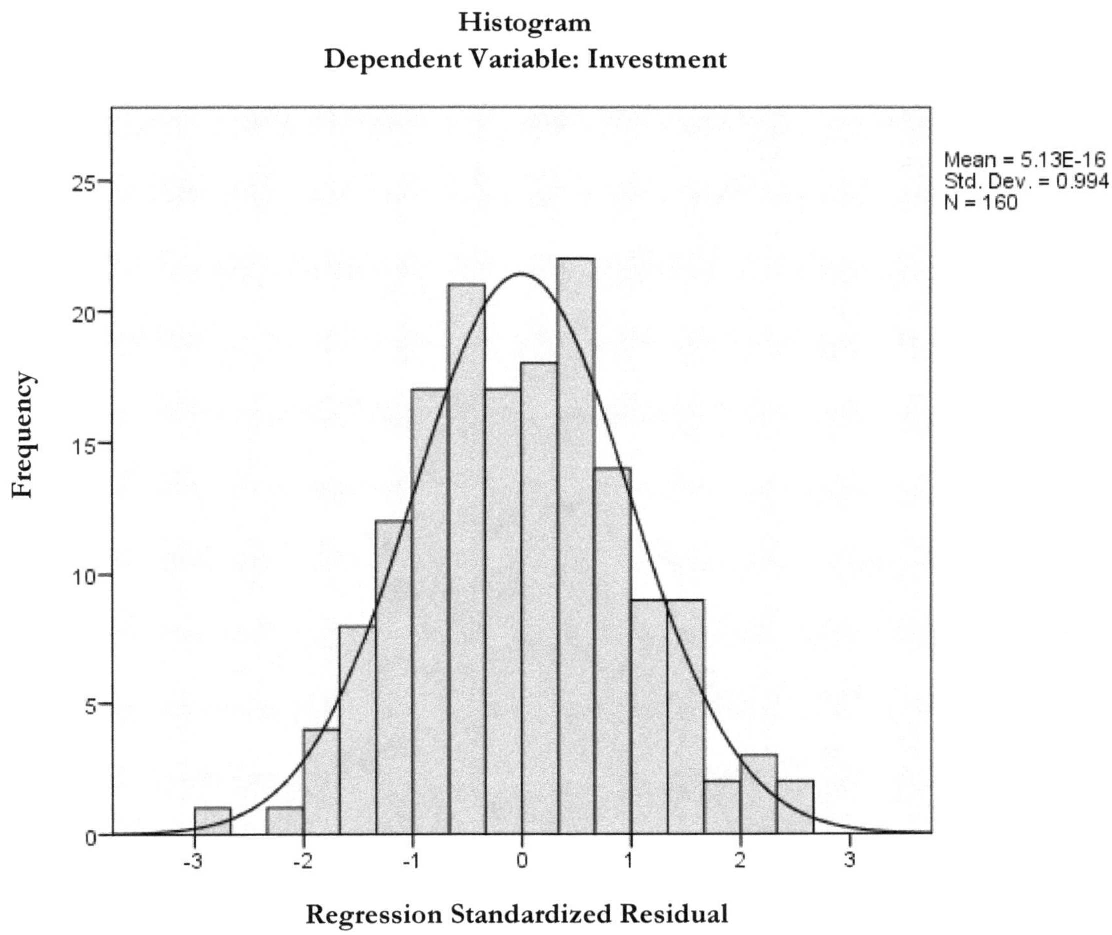

The overall model was significant, F (2, 159) = 138.475, $p < .001$. The model explained 63.8% of the variance in predicting investment ($R2 = .638$). Only online advertising ($B = 0.614, p < .001$) was a significant predictor of investment. Content marketing was not a significant predictor ($B = 0.115$, $p = .100$). An increase in online advertising results in a significant increase in investment. Table 7 provides this information.

Table 7

*Regression Coefficients of Regression Model Predicting Investment from Online Advertising and Content Marketing**

	Unstandardized Collinearity	Standardized Coefficients		t	p	Coefficients Statistics
	B	SE	β			VIF
(Constant)	.611	.128		4.772	.000	
Online	.614	.079	.676	7.824	.000	3.241
Content Marketing	.115	.070	.143	1.653	.100	3.241

*$F(2, 159) = 138.475, p < .001; R^2 = .638$

Summary

This research examined the value of investing in online advertising for customer success management (CSM) among Gen Z and its influence on their buying decisions. The main aim was to demonstrate that content marketing is a more effective strategy for engaging this young generation and establishing enduring relationships between them and investment firms. Additionally, the study sought to highlight that content marketing offers a greater return on investment and consistently drives demand for financial firms.

Four null hypotheses were addressed:

- H_{01}: Gen Z's experience with content marketing does not have a significant impact on purchase intention.
- H_{02}: Gen Z's experience with online advertising does not significantly affect purchase intention.
- H_{03}: Content marketing on a social media platform does not have a bigger role in increasing sales or strengthening investment firms' relations with Gen Z than online advertising.
- H_{04}: Online advertising is not as effective in creating demand for investment services as content marketing among Gen Z.

The results of simple and multiple regression analyses conducted with SPSS software resulted in all four null hypotheses being rejected. Thus, the study supported the following alternative hypotheses:

- H_{11}: Gen Z's experience with content marketing positively affects purchase intention.
- H_{12}: Gen Z's experience with online advertising positively affects purchase intention
- H_{13}: Content marketing in social media platforms has a bigger role in increasing sales and strengthening investment firms' relations with Gen Z than advertising.
- H_{14}: Online advertising is more effective in creating demand for investment services among Gen Z than content marketing.

Chapter V

Discussion

The data collection for this research was conducted via Survey Monkey, targeting responses from the Gen Z population, as outlined in the proposal. The data analysis involved various statistical tests, including linear regression, ANOVA, and T-test. These tests assessed the relationships between predictors and variables to determine their significance in bringing change. It is important to note that all tests assumed a linear function. Before conducting the tests, hypotheses were formulated, and assumptions were carefully reviewed to ensure the validity and reliability of the methods used.

The linear regression test analyzed one predictor variable and one dependent variable, while the ANOVA test utilized two predictor variables and one dependent variable. Meanwhile, the T-test was performed with two dependent variables and one predictor variable. The results of these tests are presented in the analysis section.

This study sought to determine the efficacy of content marketing on social media for developing and sustaining connections between investment firms and Gen Z. The results demonstrate that content marketing outperformed online advertising, consistently generating interest among Gen Z. Therefore, investment firms are likely to benefit from implementing content marketing strategies to establish enduring relationships with this demographic.

The research findings suggest that content marketing is essential for achieving a higher return on investment and securing sales. While online advertising can create demand, it does not guarantee purchases or future purchase intent. These findings indicate that businesses should adopt content marketing strategies to build long-lasting customer relationships and foster customer success management. Additionally, the results support the earlier literature, which proposed that a deeper application of content marketing tailored to customer needs and preferences is essential.

The digitally savvy nature of Gen Z means that their demand for products often begins with online research, especially given the use of artificial intelligence and increasingly targeted search engine tools. However, this generation's shorter attention span can become a challenge. The study confirmed that while multiple online offerings may create demand, they do not necessarily lead to actual purchases.

H_{01} and H_{02} in this research tested Gen Z's experience with online advertising versus content marketing on social media. Content marketing emerged as the clear winner in generating purchase intent. Moreover, content marketing is responsible for 99% of purchase intention among this generation.

H_{03} aimed to determine the impact of both content marketing and online advertising on strengthening relations with Gen Z and increasing sales. Regression test results indicate that both variables have a significant impact when increased by one unit. However, a closer analysis of the unstandardized coefficients reveals that content marketing on social media has a statistically superior positive effect on investment compared to online advertising. Specifically, content marketing had a coefficient of 0.550 ($\beta = 0.547$) and a statistically significant ($p<0.05$) effect on return on investment, while online advertising had a coefficient of 0.441 ($\beta = 0.426$). Therefore, investment firms targeting Gen Z should prioritize content marketing over online advertising to secure sales and achieve a higher return on investment.

H_{04} sought to assess whether online advertising or content marketing was more effective in generating interest in investment services among Gen Z. The regression model and T-test results indicated that both independent variables significantly impacted demand for investment services. However, the standardized coefficient (Beta) for online advertising was higher than that for content marketing in the regression model.

Furthermore, the T-test value for online advertising surpassed that of content marketing in generating demand. This implies that online investment service offerings are more likely to capture Gen Z's attention and generate initial demand.

The results may be influenced by historical events that shaped Gen Z, such as economic fluctuations, the digital environment, and the pressure for self-realization, as discussed in the literature review. The value placed on rapport and quality of information may explain the study's results (Hypothesis 4), indicating that online advertising can increase demand due to the abundance of information accessible to this technology-immersed generation. However, this does not necessarily translate into actual purchases or strong purchase intention. These results contradict from previous research, such as Wibowo et al. (2021), which indicated that online marketing alone may not be enough to drive traffic and create demand. Hypotheses 3 and 4 focus on marketing investment services and support content marketing as the clear winner for purchase intention, customer success management, and return on investment. Nevertheless, online advertising remains effective for driving traffic and increasing demand.

Content marketing on social media, represented by a coefficient of 0.550 ($\beta = 0.547$), has a statistically significant ($p<0.05$) and positive effect on investment. Hence, businesses in the investment sector should prioritize using content marketing on social media to secure and increase investment sales, rather than relying solely on online marketing. As the literature review suggested, exposure creates demand; however, content is the key to standing out amidst intense competition as firms increasingly depend on a digital rather than a physical presence in the market.

Implications of the Research for the Investment Services Sector

This research aligns with and provides valuable insights into existing literature while offering practical implications for various business sectors, particularly the investment sector. The findings reinforce the importance of adapting marketing strategies, especially content marketing, to cater to the preferences and behaviors of Generation Z.

This study highlights the value of continuous content marketing efforts, resonating with the evolving digital landscape and Gen Z's increasing reliance on online platforms. The implications extend beyond the investment sector, suggesting broader applicability for businesses targeting Gen Z consumers. While not explicitly refuting past research, these results provide a clear understanding of the effectiveness of content marketing compared to online advertising.

Addressing the project's problem statement and purpose, the research underscores the significance of allocating resources to content marketing efforts tailored to Gen Z. This aligns with the identified need to understand the preferences and behaviors of Gen Z in the context of investment services. The findings directly address the research questions and hypotheses, providing evidence that supports the notion that content marketing, especially on social media platforms, significantly impacts Gen Z's purchase intention and positively contributes to customer relations and return on investment.

In summary, the findings validate the project's purpose by offering practical guidance for businesses seeking to target Gen Z. The alignment of data collection and analysis with the problem statement and purpose is evident, as this research provides valuable insights for firm and finance professionals aiming to secure sales, manage customer relations, and remain competitive in the digital era.

Final Thoughts

It is recommended that financial investment firms, regardless of size, implement customer success management strategies, sales-driving tactics, and return-on-investment initiatives. A crucial component of these approaches should involve leveraging various social media platforms to reach Gen Z more effectively. It is essential to design customized content to establish a meaningful connection with customers, as merely generating temporary attention through online advertising is insufficient. Furthermore, staying updated with emerging marketing technologies is vital to maintaining a competitive edge.

References

Brinson, N. H., Eastin, M. S., & Cicchirillo, V. J. (2018). Reactance to personalization: Understanding the drivers behind the growth of ad blocking. Journal of Interactive Advertising, 18(2), 136-147.

https://doi.org/10.1080/15252019.2018.1491350

Field, A. (2018). Discovering statistics using IBM SPSS statistics. SAGE Publications.

Fromm, J., & Read, A. (2018). Who is Gen Z? In Marketing to Gen Z: The rules for reaching this vast--and very different--generation of influencers (pp. 1-24). AMACOM.

Grigoreva, E. A., Garifova, L. F., & Polovkina, E. A. (2021). Consumer behavior in the information economy: Generation Z. International Journal of Financial Research, 12(2),

164. https://doi.org/10.5430/ijfr.v12n2p164

Hilton, B., Hajihashemi, B., Henderson, C. M., & Palmatier, R. W. (2020). Customer success management: The next evolution in customer management practice? Industrial Marketing Management, 90, 360-369.

https://doi.org/10.1016/j.indmarman.2020.08.001

Kuazaqui, E., & Lisboa, T. C. (2019). Marketing: The Evolution of Digital Marketing. Archives of Business Research, 7(9), 89-96.

Laitkep, D., & Repkova Stofkova, K. (2021). The shopping behavior of E-commerce customers on the example of Generation Z. SHS Web of Conferences, 129, 02009.

https://doi.org/10.1051/shsconf/202112902009

Loh, S. (n.d.). Taking a survey? Your privacy concerns are answered. SurveyMonkey.

https://www.surveymonkey.co.uk/curiosity/privacy-for-survey-respondents/

Mohannad A M Abu, D., & Arqawi, S. (2020). Fintech in the eyes of Millennials and Generation Z (the financial behavior and Fintech perception). Banks and Bank Systems, 15(3), 20-28.

https://doi.org/10.21511/bbs.15(3).2020.03

Nite, J. (2018, January 8). Online marketing blog: Content marketing. ProQuest | Better research, better learning, better insights.

https://www.proquest.com/blogs-podcasts- websites/online-marketing-blog-content-evolution-5-major/doc view/1985530890/se- 2?accountid=14376

Nunnally, J. C. (1978). Psychometric theory (2nd ed.). New York: McGraw-Hill.

Pomirleanu, N., Schibrowsky, J. A., Peltier, J., & Nill, A. (2013). A review of internet marketing research over the past 20 years and future research direction. Journal of Research in Interactive Marketing, 7(3), 166-181.

https://doi.org/10.1108/JRIM-01-2013-0006

Sconti, A. (2022). Digital vs. in-person financial education: What works best for Generation Z? Journal of Economic Behavior & Organization, 194, 300-318.

https://doi.org/10.1016/j.jebo.2021.12.001

Serbetar, I., & Sedlar, I. (2016). Assessing Reliability of a Multi-Dimensional Scale by Coefficient Alpha. Revija za Elementarno Izobrazevanje, 9(1/2), 189

Sim, B. (2021, Aug 16). Fidelity on TikTok shows fierce battle for Gen-Z investors. Financial News

https://www.proquest.com/newspapers/fidelity-on-tiktok-shows-fierce-battle-gen-z/docview/2624982480/se-2

Singh, D., Katoch, R., & Singh, P. (2022). Social Media Marketing and Gen Z: A Study of Brand Attitude, Self-Brand Connection, and Purchase Intention. IUP Journal of Marketing Management, 21(3), 7-23.

https://www.proquest.com/scholarly-journals/social-media- marketing-gen-z-study-brand-attitude/ doc view/2727235958/se-2

Strozniak, P. (2022). Gen Z Is Up for Grabs. Credit Union Times,

https://www.proquest.com/trade-journals/gen-z-is-up- grabs/ doc view/2691193280/se-2

Toit, L. D. (2022). Are you ready to commit to a long-term relationship with content marketing? Bizcommunity.com.

https://www.proquest.com/other-sources/are-you-ready- commit-long-term relationship-with/ doc view/2390346647/se-2?accountid=14376

Wibowo, A., Chen, S., Wiangin, U., Ma, Y., & Ruangkanjanases, A. (2021). Customer behavior as an outcome of social media marketing: The role of social media marketing activity and customer experience. Sustainability (Basel, Switzerland), 13(1),189.

https://doi.org/10.3390/su13010189

Zoltners, A. A., Sinha, P., & Lorimer, S. E. (2019, November 18). What is a customer success manager? Harvard Business Review.

https://hbr.org/2019/11/what-is-a-customer- success-manager

www.ingramcontent.com/pod-product-compliance
Lightning Source LLC
LaVergne TN
LVHW080528210926
848481LV00022B/3647